D1391913

So long as we enjoy the light of day
may we greet one another with love.

So long as we enjoy the light of day
may we pray for one another.

Zuni

A CHILD'S BOOK OF PRAYERS

from many faiths and cultures

Compiled by Tessa Strickland

BAREFOOT BOOKS

BATH

All are nothing but flowers
in a flowering universe.

Nakagawa Soen-roshi
Zen Buddhist

Grandfather,
Look at our brokenness.

We know that in all creation
Only the human family
Has strayed from the Sacred Way.

We know that we are the ones
Who are divided
And we are the ones
Who must come back together
To walk in the Sacred Way.

Grandfather,
Sacred One,
Teach us love, compassion, and honor
That we may heal the earth
And heal each other.

Ojibwa

Air is our Master, water our father,
and the great earth our mother.
Day and night are the female and male nurses
in whose lap the whole universe plays.

Guru Nanak
Sikh

Peace is every step.
The shining red sun is my heart.
Each flower smiles with me.
How green, how fresh all that grows.
How cool the wind blows.
Peace is every step.
It turns the endless path to joy.

Thich Nhat Hanh
Zen Buddhist

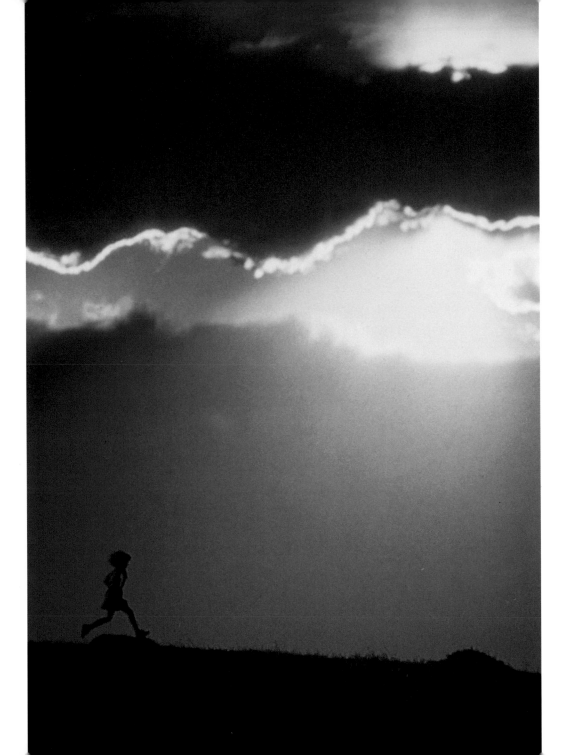

Earth teach me stillness
    as the grasses are stilled with light.
Earth teach me suffering
    as old stones suffer with memory.
Earth teach me humility
    as blossoms are humble with beginning.
Earth teach me caring
    as the mother who secures her young.
Earth teach me courage
    as the tree which stands all alone.
Earth teach me limitation
    as the ant which crawls on the ground.
Earth teach me freedom
    as the eagle which soars in the sky.
Earth teach me resignation
    as the leaves which die in the fall.
Earth teach me regeneration
    as the seed which rises in the spring.
Earth teach me to forget myself
    as melted snow forgets its life.
Earth teach me to remember kindness
    as dry fields weep with rain.

Ute

Blessed art Thou, O Lord our God,
King of the universe,
who makest the bands of sleep
to fall upon mine eyes
and slumber upon mine eyelids.

May it be Thy will, O Lord my God,
and God of my fathers,
to suffer me to lie down in peace
and to let me rise up again in peace.

Jewish

Now I lay me down to sleep.
I pray Thee, Lord, my soul to keep.
Your love be with me through the night
And wake me with the morning light.

Christian

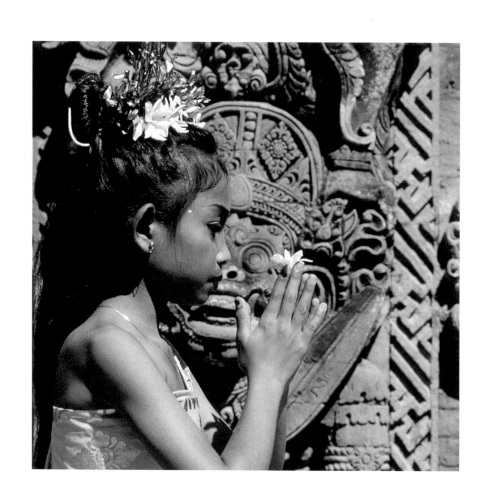

NOTES ON THE PRAYERS

Editor's note: This book reaches across many traditions and cultures, but, inevitably, not all traditions could be included. The photographs and prayers were selected and combined to convey the universality of spiritual experience among the world's peoples. Out of respect for the Islamic faith, Muslim prayers were omitted because the Islamic tradition does not make use of visual images.

The notes below follow the order of the prayers in the book. It is hoped that adults will use these notes to help young readers achieve a greater understanding of the prayers.

Zuni prayer: The opening prayer is taken from the ancient *Night Chant of the Zuni*, which has been intoned for centuries by the indigenous people of the southwestern United States. The night chant celebrates the power of light, both in a physical sense, as the sun whose power ensures the warmth and light necessary for living things to grow, and in a spiritual sense, as the light whose power banishes the darkness of ignorance, giving us a greater awareness of our true nature. The theme of light (symbolized by the sun) as the dispeller of ignorance is common to religious traditions throughout the world.

Russian Orthodox prayer: An ancient Christian faith, the Russian Orthodox religion places great emphasis on the appreciation of beauty in nature, music, and art. This tradition also places the highest value on prayer and its relevance to every aspect of daily life. This prayer connects our everyday activities and the rhythms of the natural world with the rhythms of our inner life.

Unitarian prayer: The Unitarian tradition offers individuals a way to discover wholeness and a sense of underlying unity in life by understanding that truth comes to us from many different sources, especially from our own life experience. This prayer expresses the Unitarian reverence for the earth and the value placed on sharing and on openness to the beliefs of others.

Christian prayer: The idea that each of us has a guardian angel to help us on our journey through life is a traditional belief of the Catholic faith, but it may well have roots that reach back before Christianity, since the idea of spirit guides or guardians is common to many ancient cultures.

The Bhairava Yamala: The numerous gods and goddesses of the Hindu tradition represent the many ways in which we perceive and experience the divine. In India, the divine was originally seen as maternal. Excerpted from an ancient Hindu scripture, *The Bhairava Yamala*, this prayer celebrates the divine mother's awesome power, which radiates throughout the manifest world. The light of the divine mother represents not only physical light as we perceive it, but also the energy that enlightens consciousness and vitalizes all living things.

Nakagawa Soen-roshi: Nakagawa Soen-roshi was one of the first Zen teachers to introduce Buddhism to the West. Zen is a Japanese school of Buddhism that does not separate the sacred from the secular. It focuses on simplicity and on a life which is in harmony with nature. Along with describing a particular moment in summer, this poem celebrates the continual flowering of energy throughout the universe.

Ojibwa prayer: An indigenous people of North America, the Ojibwa live in parts of the northern United States and southern Canada. For the Ojibwa and other Native Americans, sacred teachings are expressed in the laws of nature, and the natural world is considered to be the dwelling place of the Great Spirit. According to Native American belief, contentment and well-being are possible only if we follow the Sacred Way of nature.

Jewish prayer: This celebratory prayer is traditionally recited each year at the first blossoming of trees in spring.

Tewa Pueblo prayer: The Tewa are one of the many Pueblo communities who inhabit the southwestern United States. Family is the cornerstone of Tewa culture, but all humans are also seen as children of the earth as mother and the sky as father. This prayer shows the Tewa's profound respect for the beauty and mystery of the natural world and the importance they place on living in harmony with nature.

Zhuangzi: Zhuangzi lived in the fourth century B.C. and is one of the fathers of Taoism, China's oldest religion. This prayer is recorded in his book of essays, also named *Zhuangzi*, one of the classic texts of Taoism, which regards harmony between humans and the laws of nature as a spiritual ideal.

Christian prayer: Many prayers acknowledge the interdependence of human beings and the forces of nature. This simple Christian grace acknowledges that interdependence by connecting the sweetness of the food we eat with the sweetness of the living world.

Guru Nanak: In the fifteenth century, Guru Nanak founded Sikhism in northern India. Living in troubled times between Hindus and Muslims, he encouraged people to see beyond their religious differences and to have a sense of justice and social responsibility. He taught through poetry and practical example, and his verse forms part of the *Guru Granth Sahib*, a collection of poetry that Sikhs revere and recite from daily.

Thich Nhat Hanh: Thich Nhat Hanh is a Vietnamese Buddhist monk, scholar, poet, and peace activist. Exiled from his country for his peaceful resistance to the Vietnam War, he now lives with the community he founded at Plum Village, Meyrac, France, where he teaches, writes, and gardens. He continues to help Vietnamese refugees and leads retreats in mindful living all over the world. This prayer helps us to understand that peace is not only a social and spiritual ideal; it is also our natural state.

Ute prayer: The Ute are a small, formerly nomadic tribe living in the southwestern United States. For the Ute, as for other Native Americans, the earth must not be controlled or changed, for it is intrinsically beautiful, harmonious, and sacred. If we know how to relate properly to the earth, it will teach us everything we need to know.

Numbers: *Numbers* is one of the five books of Moses, known collectively as the Pentateuch. It contains a series of instructions given to Moses by God. This blessing is an extremely powerful prayer because, in Judaism, normally it is thought impossible to look upon the face of God and survive.

Jewish prayer: This traditional nighttime prayer asks for peace during the hours of sleep and acknowledges the power of God both as the provider of sleep and restorer of wakefulness. The quality of energy at dawn and dusk make these significant times for prayer in many traditions.

Christian prayer: This children's prayer is part of Christianity's oral tradition. In simple verse, it expresses the willing surrender of the individual to the divine, giving a special quality to the moments between wakefulness and sleep.

For my children—T.S.

The barefoot child symbolises the human being whose natural integrity and capacity for action are unimpaired. In this spirit, Barefoot Books publishes new and traditional myths, stories, poems and fairy tales whose themes demonstrate the pitfalls and dangers that surround our progress through life: the qualities that are needed to face and overcome those dangers; and the equal importance of action and reflection in doing so. Our intention is to present stories from a wide range of cultures in such a way as to delight and inspire readers of all ages while honouring the tradition from which the story has been inherited.

For a Barefoot Books catalogue, please write to Barefoot Books Ltd, PO Box 95, Kingswood, Bristol BS15 5BH.

SOURCES AND ACKNOWLEDGEMENTS

Many thanks to everyone who helped in the creation of A Child's Book of Prayers, in particular to Andrea Andriotto and Caroline English, for painstaking picture research; to Tom Grzelinksi, who learnt that book design is not always as straightforward as it seems; to Gopinder Panesar and Nancy Traversy of Barefoot Books and to Helen Sweetland of Sierra Club Books for Children, San Francisco.

The Photographs

Grateful acknowledgement is made to the following picture libraries and photographers for their permission to reproduce material copyrighted or controlled by them:

© **Robert Harding Picture Library:** for child in swing, USA (p. 10), and children holding hands, USA (p. 22).
© **The Image Bank:** for child running into the sunset (p. 30).
© **Don Klumpp, The Image Bank:** for girl wading into the ocean, Mexico (jacket, p. 1 and p. 26).
© **Sandra Lousada, Collections:** for two children hugging, England (p. 2 and p. 32).
© **Edwin Maynard, The Tibet Image Bank:** for butterlamps, Tibet (p. 34).
© **Nock, Hutchison Picture Library:** for Kogi Steps, Colombia (p. 4 and p. 16).
© **Pictor International:** for Peruvian father with child (p. 20).
© **G.A. Rossi, The Image Bank:** for Balinese girl in temple (p. 12 and p. 38).
© **Irene Slegt, The Tibet Image Bank:** for monks blowing horns, Tibet (p. 8).
© **Sobel & Klonsky, The Image Bank:** for young farm girl riding horse cart, USA (p. 6).
© **Topham PicturePoint:** for boy with bowl of fish, Zaire (p. 24).
© **Jenny Woodcock, Reflections Photolibrary, Bath:** child with cherry blossoms, England (p. 18), and for child sleeping, England (p. 36).
© **David Woodfall, Woodfall Wild Images:** for traditional hay meadow, England (p. 14).
© **Yan Lun Jean Yves, The Image Bank:** for Chinese children in rice field (p. 28).

The Prayers

Grateful acknowledgement is made to the following authors and publishers for permission to reprint material copyrighted by them:

William Collins Sons & Co. Ltd for excerpt from The Bible: Revised Standard Version. Copyright © 1973 by Division of Christian Education of the National Council of the Churches of Christ in the United States of America.

Harper San Francisco for an excerpt from The Name of My Beloved: Verses of the Sikh Gurus, translated and introduced by Nikki-Gurinder Kaur Singh (1995).

An excerpt from The Long Road Turns to Joy: A Guide to Walking Meditation by Thich Nhat Hanh (1996), reprinted with the permission of Parallax Press, Berkeley, California.

University of Chicago Press for an excerpt from The Tewa World by Alfonso Ortiz copyright © 1964 by University of Chicago Press. All rights reserved.

The publishers have made every effort to contact holders of copyright material. If you have not received our correspondence, please contact us for inclusion in future editions.